ONE+ONE>2

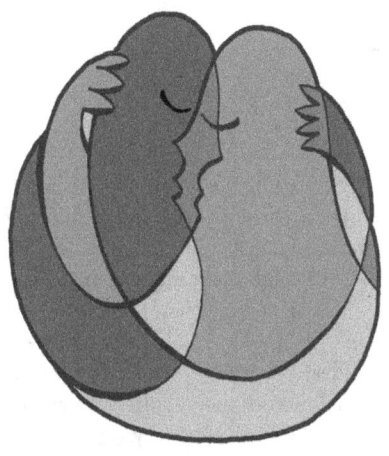

The Online Dating Guide for Women Over 50

CHRISTIANE HILE

PUBLISHED BY FIDELI PUBLISHING, INC.

One + One > 2

Copyright © 2019 Christiane Hile

All rights reserved. No part of this book may be used or reproduced by any means, graphic, electronic, or mechanical, including photocopying, recording, taping or by any information storage retrieval system without the written permission of the publisher except in the case of brief quotations embodied in critical articles and reviews.

Events portrayed did take place. However, all of the characters names plus several incidents, organizations, geographic, chronological and identifying details have been changed to protect privacy.

Books may be ordered through booksellers or by contacting:

Fideli Publishing, Inc.
119 W Morgan St.
Martinsville, IN 46151
888-343-3542
www.FideliPublishing.com

Cover imagery © lucamendieta/stock.adobe.com.

ISBN: 978-1-948638-35-7 (soft cover)
ISBN: 978-1-948638-36-4 (hardcover)

Printed in the United States of America.

*In loving memory of Robert (Bob) Raos
and Barry Robert Hile.*

TABLE OF CONTENTS

Introduction.. vii

Chapter 1 **Getting Started**... 1
One Arrow in Your Quiver........................... 3
Logic over Stigma 5
Pick a Paid Site.. 8
Get Clear on Critical Qualities 9

Chapter 2 **Writing Your Profile** 17
Telling Your Story.. 17
Managing Filters and Connections.......... 20
Experiment 26
Deal Killers.. 28

Chapter 3 **Selecting Appropriate Representative Photos**............................ 31

Chapter 4 **Screening Candidates By Phone** 37
Push to the Phone....................................... 37
Limit Texting... 44

Chapter 5 **Dealing with Scammers and Jerks**......... 47
Scammers 47
Jerks 52

Chapter 6 **Target: Meeting Eight Men in Person** ... 55

Chapter 7 **Practice the Three-Date Rule**................. 61

Chapter 8	**Navigating First Dates** 67
	Mindset.. 67
	Safety 69
	More Tips 69
	Ghosting 75
Chapter 9	**Second Date Diva Dinner** 79
Chapter 10	**The Third Date** 83
	You're the Host... 83
	"Go/No-Go" Decision................................ 87
	Uncoupling 88
	Sex 91
	Disclosure Dilemma 95
Chapter 11	**Reaching the One Year Milestone** 99
	Relationship Housekeeping 99
	What to Call Each Other....................... 101
	Sashay and Savor 102
	Date Nights.. 103
Chapter 12	**Breaking Up and Taking a Break**.......107
	Fatal Flaws... 107
	How to Uncouple and Mean It 108
	He Breaks Up 110
	Take a Break.. 111
Chapter 13	**Now You Have Game** 113
	Endnotes... 119
	Acknowledgements 123
	About the Author 125

INTRODUCTION

When I was 48, my husband died unexpectedly. It was only 36 days from the day of his devastating cancer diagnosis to his passing. Throughout our 10 years together, we'd been deeply in love. Both of us worked in technology — he was a mechanical engineer and I was in marketing for a software company that serves small business customers. As avid skiers and sailing travelers, we enjoyed an exceptionally harmonious relationship and it seemed to me that our life was much bigger than I ever imagined it would be. It was as if one + one > 2!

At 50, I sold our home in Calabasas, California, and moved into a Craftsman house in Houston's historic Heights neighborhood.

Houston surprised me. It turned out to have a bursting-at-the-seams food scene, bike trails and plenty of opera, ballet and theater. It also has a good male to female ratio, since it's filled with well-traveled oil industry geologists and engineers and a good bunch of medical professionals servicing the Texas Medical Center, the largest conglomerate of health care institutions in the world.

Let's face it — numbers matter! I know because I grew up in Victoria, B.C., Canada, a picturesque government retiree town notorious for having a 2:1 female to male ratio. Men don't even have to "try" there. Fish jump onto their hooks before they even cast a line.

I met my husband through a singles ski club before internet dating became mainstream, but many of our friends met online through Match.com. Platforms like Match, eHarmony, JDate and OurTime established themselves as paid sites, while free sites like Plenty of Fish (POF), OkCupid, Coffee Meets Bagel, Tinder and many more followed. Although happily married, I was intrigued by the online dating trend because it seemed like a magical intersection between math and romance. As a criminal defense lawyer for 10 years and then a market researcher, I've long been interested in human behavior especially how maturity changes us. So, I was very curious about online dating and whether it was working as intended.

Eventually, it was my time to move on from what had been my previous married life. I figured that I'd write my "what I want in a relationship" wish list and with a sprinkling of time and a business-like methodology, the "right-fit" partner would eventually emerge through dating. To help gauge this process and the potential variables, I created a rudimentary spreadsheet. I confess that I can be a hardcore pragmatist but, as a Virgo, I'm also a romantic. And remember, I'd been a market researcher. At the very least, I had a burning desire to track how many men I needed to meet before a right-fit partner came along. And if the first right-fit didn't work out, I planned to refine and repeat the process.

I was also curious about how dating in midlife would differ from dating when I was in my 20s and 30s. As I came to terms with "maturing" in my 50's, I sensed that dating might become more challenging at some point. Yet I am surrounded by examples of vibrant 70-, 80- and even 90-something women who continue to lead extraordinarily active lives. A number of acquaintances and friends in their 70's teach, lead companies or run professional practices, working full time. One 86-year-old girl friend is authoring her fifth book while continuing to work with psychotherapy patients. Dr. Ruth Westheimer, who turned 90 in 2018, is still speaking and writing books about sex and at 92, Queen Elizabeth continues to weigh in on national decisions and open Parliament each year.

My mom flat out told me that aging sucks (she used another word). I knew a few acquaintances who were struggling with aging in various ways, and sadly I know of one who didn't make it through midlife. A barrage of self-defeating beliefs about romance blew my way, too. My doctor explained that *all* her single, menopausal patients have told her "men our age want much younger women." My father said that at my age, "the good ones are all taken."

Worried about whether I was going to find a ski partner again, I was also anxious by the seemingly unavoidable possibility that Chico's would be my future clothier. Girlfriends were getting Botox, face-lifts, tummy tucks and lots of cool sculpting sessions. I began to make frequent trips to consult doctors and nutritionists about losing the additional 20 pounds that graced the pear-shaped part of my body suddenly. I was told that I needed to make the gym my "third space" to ensure I worked out six times per week if I was truly serious about retaining my figure.

Determined to learn something about the lesser known aspects of midlife, I was eager to get firsthand knowledge about dating instead of hearing about what it was and wasn't from others. I also wanted the chance to see it from men's perspectives. So, while I was sincerely interested in dating, I added a loose layer of market research methodology. Essentially, I set out with a businesslike approach to "work through the numbers" while having social "adventures" meeting interesting men. I resolved not to overinvest emotionally in any one man until I was sure that he was a "right fit." But I was going to have fun if I could.

Regardless of how you arrive at this juncture in your romantic lives, if you're reading this book then you've likely decided that you would like to find a special person to love and share the rest of your life with. I wrote this book because I found that so many accomplished, single women I've spoken with, want to meet someone significant but are reluctant to start with or stick to a disciplined dating approach. They postpone dating until some milestone is reached such as losing weight or they guffaw at how much time it takes, giving up after only one disappointing experience.

Many women simply don't know what to expect from dating or how to show up for it. They never dated or if they did, it was eons ago. I've also witnessed confident, proactive "wonder women" who whack their way through dating like scything through a cornfield, meeting many men but only "once" because there was no chemistry on the first coffee date. Then they peter out from dating fatigue, declaring to all who will listen, "Online dating doesn't work!"

And, lastly, let's face it. Wisps of an online dating stigma still exist in baby boomer and older generations. That isn't true for Millennials or post-Millennials who have grown up with smart technology and intuitively understand the efficiency of online platforms.

Almost all of us have battle scars from bumps along the way, causing us to be a bit more risk adverse than we were 20 or 30 years ago. But, overall, we are much more intuitive and discerning. Yes, dating can be complicated now that we have to reckon with opinionated, grown children, pay down post-divorce debts or assist end-of–life parents. We need two pairs of eyeglasses at any given time, we're peeing more frequently and sleeping less. And, frankly, I can't stand gratuitous violence and sex on TV anymore. Nope, I didn't watch *Game of Thrones*.

My online dating journey turned out to be rich and filled with as much self-discovery as it was with rare insights about men's journeys. Plus, dating accelerated getting to know my city — those hard-to-find special spots such as small jazz joints, blues brunch places,

Introduction

obscure festivals or private associations that quietly underpin a city beneath the transient and commercial traffic. I still feel uniquely privileged and stronger because of my dating experiences.

Most importantly though, life is magical when we share laughter and tears with someone who "gets" us. Our hearts long for deep connection.

This book is for ladies who aspire to find their "sweetheart."

Since almost 40% of heterosexual couples now meet online, my hope is that this book helps you expand or accelerate your dating journey to find your right-fit man.[1] At the very least, try out these seven easy guidelines and see how it goes:

1. Use a **paid** dating site.
2. Push to the **phone**, limit texting.
3. **Meet eight** men in person.
4. Commit to **3 dates**.
5. Be your **best self**, every time.
6. Let him take the **lead**.
7. Pressure-test a **right-fit** relationship for up to **one year.**

CHAPTER 1

GETTING STARTED

ONLINE DATING INCREASES THE ODDS

If you want to find a special man to spend the second half of your life with, and if you're clear about the qualities in him that are important to you, then online apps need to be in your quiver of dating resources. They increase the odds of meeting your future sweetheart even if you end up meeting him offline. It's simple math.

Meeting via dating sites now surpasses more traditionally popular means of introduction, including through family and friends. Almost 40% of straight

Almost 40% of straight couples now meet online.[1]

couples now meet online.[1] Online dating use among midlife adults in their 50s and 60s has risen substantially[2]; more than 28 percent of Match members are 50 to 74 years old, and 91 percent have attended college.[3]

Zoosk has over 40 million profiles worldwide.[4] And did I mention that more men than women use dating apps?[5] When you use dating sites, you'll see a larger sample of available men than you could ever connect with at the grocery store or in church.

You will be exposed to a large number of single men in your age bracket who are looking for a romantic partner. It's common sense if you stop to consider that, like you, many men are dealing with a combination of issues ranging from traveling for work, recovering from the death of a spouse or from divorce, or simply overcoming the mental hurdle of feeling like they're not sure that dating thing works these days.

Plus, online dating is more convenient. Consider the case of Dan, an introspective, thoughtful commercial airline pilot in his early 50s who loves to read New Age teachings and has a penchant for fine wine. He's long been collecting Bordeaux and now has a remarkable collection. He's also the noncustodial dad of an athletic 14-year-old in the Pacific Northwest, devoted to taking his son to swim meets, birthday parties and basketball practice. Dan wanted nothing more than to meet a single mom to share family activities, romantic evenings and travel adventures.

A heavy flight load and the complexity of parenting didn't provide enough chances for him to forge new relationships by attending local fundraisers or singles dinner parties. Online dating let him do his research while he was traveling for work. He found time to initiate phone conversations from his hotel room and then carved out "dates" in the cities where he had the most layovers. He was able to cast a wider geographic net because of his job-related mobility.

He now has two de facto homes — a rental house in the Pacific Northwest where he stays when it's "his" weekend with his son and a home shared with his girlfriend in the Southwest, where he spends most of his spare time. They met online.

ONE ARROW IN YOUR QUIVER

Online dating doesn't preclude the possibility of meeting someone offline through lucky happenstance or a friend's introduction. So, don't stop asking friends for help with introductions to eligible bachelors. Online dating is not an either/or proposition. It's just "one" arrow in your dating quiver. Meeting someone

Online dating is not an either/or proposition. It's just "one" arrow in your dating quiver.

through work or community affiliations and at fundraisers, sports events or country clubs is still a great way to meet like-minded men, too!

Keep going to bike rallies, volunteer events, memoir writing classes, golf tournaments, dog parks, car shows, BBQ cooking demonstrations, other peoples' weddings, school reunions, yoga classes, etc. Go alone and strike up conversations. Join a singles ski club, sign up for dance lessons, learn how to shoot clay pigeons, try AirBnB Experiences like dinner parties or kayaking, cycle in a neighborhood charity fundraiser and keep an eye out at work.

What about professional matchmakers? I considered using one myself at the outset but abandoned the notion. I didn't have confidence that matchmakers have sufficient inventory for me. They typically only provide their clients with three to five dates over the course of six months to a year, fewer for midlife women.[6]

Plus, no one knows you and your evolving dating wish list better than you, so how can a personalized matchmaking service be more efficient than the digital realm? My analogy was real estate. I've found my last three homes myself using online tools, even though I was working with a realtor. Matchmaking seems like a vocation that, like selling residential real estate, is fraying. It doesn't make much sense anymore because it's too inefficient and expensive.

Although I think that a dedicated, persuasive matchmaker could have convinced me to be more open to meeting someone I wouldn't normally have considered, I also opted out because of the high cost. The price tag can be somewhere between $5,000 and $50,000.[7]

LOGIC OVER STIGMA

The thought of online dating is "scary" for many people, especially for mature singles. Incredulously, some men and women still disdainfully imply that online dating is for some sort of illusory category of folks who inhabit the margins of family-centric or socially-minded mainstream communities. Others

"Tinderize" the process, suggesting that most online dating sites are used by men just looking for a hookup (sex), nothing serious.

I repeatedly fell into conversations in which I felt "shamed" for my enthusiasm about online dating, and this stigma came my way from both men and women. A typical case in point is Cullen, a former colleague, who scrunched up his face when I told him I was online dating. Although we both worked in technology and clearly understood the power of numbers, he still declared,

"I'm so grateful not to have to do THAT!"

When he said that, I felt demeaned. Here I was — a working professional with many hobbies and a solid "happy marriage" track record under my belt. Why wouldn't I want to increase the odds of meeting a compatible, single man? And why wouldn't I want to enjoy the process of meeting someone like that? Millennials consider it natural and have much success with it. How could online dating not make sense for me?

Cullen's attitude is neither rational nor pragmatic. In fact, it smacks of binariness — thinking there is only a right and a wrong way to do things. If you can't have it, the next best mode of thought is to convince

Getting Started

yourself that it's not worth having. So, just ignore comments like his.

And, by the way, also ignore the warning that midlife, single men just want to connect with a much younger woman. Many don't! Middle-aged men are often scared, too, climbing up and out of a midlife odyssey of their own, whether by way of an expensive divorce, death of a spouse or parent or cancer scare. Many wonder whether they still "have game" and can even still get it up. You'd be surprised about the number of single men in your peer group who want to meet someone just like you!

If you like meeting interesting people, dressing up a little (or a lot), going out and exploring new places, then dating can be really fun. It is work — no doubt about that. Sometimes it stings, but all in all it can be a joyful journey. Plus, you'll learn, learn, learn ... about

Middle-aged men are often scared too, climbing up and out of a midlife odyssey of their own.

yourself, your city and men in the second half of their lives.

PICK A PAID SITE

Pick a paid site to start. With paid sites, subscribers have to put a stake in the ground by pulling out their credit card. Someone who can't afford to buy you dinner or worse, someone who is married, often won't pay for a dating site either.

I tried a few free sites. OkCupid, for example, was uniquely fun. At the beginning, it develops a psychological persona based on a never-ending list of personal questions that you can answer while standing in line at the DMV. I also successfully used Bumble, the so-called "feminist app," where women have to make the first move. Generally speaking though, the problem with free sites is that they have a low barrier to entry. This means that you have to work harder weeding through a wider range of people that may include more married men, lookie-loos and cheapskates. Pause and reconsider if you find yourself in an extended digital flirt on a free dating site with a guy who suddenly disappears. He was probably already in a relationship, and possibly even married.

Try to use sites that require a written profile and attribute preferences in addition to photos. There's no guarantee that the profiles are necessarily thoughtful or honest — some posting the briefest, most clichéd write-ups. However, the act of writing your own profile helps you focus and sharpen your intentions about what you want and don't want.

When I became serious about meeting someone, I chose Match because it's a paid site, it's the most well-known platform,[8] and it requires profiles extensive enough to put off casual dilettantes.

GET CLEAR ON CRITICAL QUALITIES

Outline what you're looking for in a relationship to lay the foundation for writing your profile. Start by listing the "**feelings**" that must ultimately be present **for you** if you end up together. As an example, I shared my list below.

When we are together I feel:

- He **adores** me just the way I am;
- He would **take good care of me** if I ever got sick;
- He **has my back** and I never worry about what he's up to when we're apart;

- He **understands me**, so I can easily share ideas and don't have to edit myself or over-explain when we have discussions; and
- When it comes to **money,** he's responsible, transparent and we have similar values.

Building on this list of feelings, add your list of "**he must…**" attributes. These are attributes that simply must exist **in him** because you can't live without them. For me, the list looked like this:

He must:

- **Like dogs,** since having a Standard Poodle is a non-negotiable for me;
- **Enjoy exercising** outdoors, because cycling, hiking or kayaking journeys and shared adventure trips are essential to my soul;
- Be a **nonsmoker** and **responsible drinker,** because I can't stand the smell of cigarette smoke and don't want to worry about DUIs or worse;
- Be **financially self-sufficient** (have a job or pension, own a business or otherwise have enough capital to support himself), because I

want to be able to continue my lifestyle at its current level;

- Have good **phone etiquette**, putting his phone away during conversations and meals; and
- Be able to **get us a table** in a crowded bar with verve.

I'm a bit embarrassed to add this last requirement because it doesn't seem to have the same weight as the others, but I stand by it. It's my way of gauging a man's confidence and resourcefulness. It's also my shorthand way of measuring testosterone. I confess that in several past long-term relationships, I was often the one to lead the chicken-hawk scout for a table in a busy lounge. One of my exes even insisted that I be the one to get our drinks at a crowded bar, saying that as a woman I'd get served faster than he would, even though I had to step up on the kick rail just to be seen among the tall guys ordering drinks for their sweethearts. It's a bit nit-picky, but I'm seriously done doing that. A man can make me swoon by saying:

"Wait here for a sec. I'll get us a table…what would you like to drink?"

One + One >2

After listing feelings that you're looking to experience, and must-have attributes, make a third list — the one that you would usually start with — the one that says, "tall, dark and handsome." Just be absolutely sure that this third list really contains "essentials" and not "nice to haves." Just because you "required" a clean-shaven man with a flat stomach who weighed at least 50 pounds more than you when you were 22, doesn't mean that you need that now.

Also, a man in love is a man whose appearance can be tweaked, within reason. A beard can be trimmed, the right jacket can transform a portly man into a distinguished one, and a balding man can transform into a steamy stunner once convinced to shave his head bald. On the other hand, if you really can't put up with a hairy back because your smarmy Uncle Pete had one, then put "hairless back" as an essential on your list.

When I was in my 20s, I had a thing for tall men — the taller, the better — to the point where I even dated my girlfriend's brother, who was 6 feet 6 inches tall. We tried to dance once. I spent the three minutes that we shuffled around the floor staring at his upper abdomen. After meeting my late husband who was 5 feet 11 inches, I completely changed my mind about height requirements. Now, it's 5 feet 6 inches to 6 feet, because

Getting Started

I love to dance and steal kisses unexpectedly. Stealing kisses is hard to do when you need an elevator to get up to his lips.

Lastly, a bit about ethnic, cultural, political and religious alignment. Be real versus politically correct here. If you're Jewish and you know that you will never feel the full breadth of a forever love relationship if he doesn't value celebrating Rosh Hashanah with you, make being Jewish and observing Jewish Holy Days a requirement. Don't kid yourself.

Nina, a divorced South Asian-American, single mother who stridently considered herself open to dating a man regardless of race or religion, joined a matchmaking service. The service arranged lunch with a handsome African-American physician. When she first entered the restaurant for lunch and saw him, she had a "moment" … one of those pauses where she caught herself, surprised by her sudden irrational reticence. But she ended up jumping in and had a lovely conversation over lunch.

The physician asked her out again via text, suggesting a specific date. When she replied with alternate dates since the date that he'd proposed conflicted with Diwali, he texted back, "What's Diwali?"

She explained that it's the Hindu Festival of Lights.

"Do you mean you're not Christian?" he asked.

"Correct, I'm Hindu," she explained.

He then broke it off saying that he was only interested in dating Christian women.

After recovering from the rejection, she had a good laugh about the irony of how this dating encounter played out. Despite the break-off, he had helped her pressure test her elasticity around diversity in the dating realm and experience what it was like to be passed over as a result of religious misalignment. In the end, she met, dated and happily married a Presbyterian.

To help you avoid scenarios like Nina's, compile a chart similar to the one below to help define what you're looking for.

YOUR REQUIRED FEELINGS	HIS CRITICAL QUALITIES	HIS VALUE ALIGNMENT
I must feel he'll keep my secrets	He must enjoy and respect my children	He welcomes friends & family into his home during the Holidays
I must feel safe with him	He must like my pets	Voting and civic duty are important to him
I must feel adored and loved by him	He must enjoy at least two of the same outdoor activities that I do	He is a political moderate who respects different points of view
I must feel understood by him	He must drink moderately	He will gladly go to my church with me at least for Easter & Christmas

CHAPTER 2

WRITING YOUR PROFILE

TELLING YOUR STORY

The care and attention that you devote to your profile and photos can be defining. From a heart and soul perspective, the act of writing your profile marks the most tangible starting point in your journey towards finding a wonderful man. There's an art to striking a balance between saying just enough to capture the right man's attention, and saying too much by pouring your heart out and coming across as jaded, needy or indiscriminate.

Keep the tone of your story fairly general while offering sufficient detail about your values and lifestyle to enable men to quickly see whether you'd be a good fit for them or not and vice versa. Craft an upbeat description of yourself with fun specifics that don't compromise your privacy; e.g., "I've explored Appalachia and

One + One >2

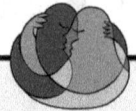

The act of writing your profile marks the most tangible starting point in your journey towards finding a wonderful man.

am hoping to trek Machu Picchu soon," instead of "I like hiking." Include humor to show that you don't take yourself too seriously and that you're approachable. I started my profile with this paragraph:

"I ski in storms, will run in the rain, and I can get ready to go anywhere faster than you can."

If you think that my opening line probably intimidated some wonderful men who don't ski, you'd be right. I later realized that the ski reference narrowed my dating pool too much. Going solo on two annual ski trips with a local ski club would scratch my annual ski itch, so I deleted the ski reference and changed "run" to "walk" because many of us now have knee problems. That doesn't mean we don't exercise. I kept the spirit of this sentence to amplify that I was looking for an outdoorsy man, one who appreciates a woman who can dash out without worrying about makeup and hair if it's warranted.

Don't get specific about where you live or work, taking care to protect your privacy. And please do not write that you're "selective." It's completely redundant because everyone feels this way, not just you.

Here are some writing guidelines to help you get started:

DO's

- Express grounded confidence by sharing a few defining achievements; e.g., "Raised two children successfully, launched and built a professional career in healthcare."

- Spark curiosity creatively; e.g., "I can show you hidden ethnic eatery gems even though meatloaf is my best dish," instead of, "I'm a meat and potatoes type of cook."

- Share a vision of how he fits in to your life; e.g., "We both like to bundle up for motorcycle journeys through the Blue Ridge Mountains, trailer out to NASCAR races and read the *New York Times* in bed on rainy Sunday mornings."

DON'Ts

- Don't say that your children (or cats) come first. Most men will admire the fact that your children are a top priority but it's table stakes for most higher-functioning folks. It's not romantic to point out to someone that he comes second.

- Don't be a "Negative Nellie" by offering a list of men who you don't want to meet; e.g., "unemployed," "nonbeliever," "not into exercise," etc. If you indicated that working out was important when you indicated your preferences or if your profile says that you work out three times a week, there's no need to say it again in a negative way.

- Don't reveal how long you've been dating and avoid the image of a seasoned, dating battle ax; e.g., do not write, "Here I go again … back on Match after a year of this dating thing."

MANAGING FILTERS AND CONNECTIONS

Filters are attributes that software developers use to define a universe of data. It sounds technical but the bottom line is that filters are levers that you can

Writing Your Profile

turn on or off. They are the essential ingredients for building behind-the-scene data personas that help you get "matched." You can adjust those levers, thereby tweaking your persona from time to time so that you increase (or decrease) the number of potential, compatible matches that you get.

Ultimately, you are in charge of your online dating experience, though. It's like using a fishing net to catch fish. The bigger the net, the more fish you'll catch. Sorting through all those fish to find the perfect keeper takes time. If your filters are too porous, you'll waste a lot of time sorting and you'll probably get dating fatigue.

For example, if you don't specify that you would like to meet someone in the 55- to 65-year-old age range, you might get too many inquiries. Getting a lot of attention can seem like fun at first but it quickly

Your online profile is like using a fishing net to catch fish. The bigger the net, the more fish you'll catch.

morphs into decision paralysis and exhaustion. If you're connecting with too many men and feel overwhelmed, try reducing your geographic radius from 50 miles to 10 miles, for example.

On the other hand, if you make your filters too narrow, you'll quickly exhaust your dating candidate inventory. If you stipulate in your preferences that you are only interested in tall Catholic men who live within a 5-mile radius, your inventory might soon be too scarce. If you're not seeing enough candidates, try loosening your filters. The good news is that on most sites you can experiment by contracting and expanding filters (geographic radius, age range, religion, etc.). And I'll add that there's absolutely no reason not to loosen your age filter "down" to include younger men.

Women complain about the scarcity of peer-aged men who are active, engaged and willing to step out beyond the sofa and the television's football game. In lowered voices they also complain about impotence. Although not essential to every romantic partnership, a healthy sex life is beneficial for physical health, self-esteem and the emotional bond shared in an intimate relationship.

While couples can continue to enjoy sex into their 80s and beyond, men's sexual function can sharply decrease after age 50, especially with physical inactivity, alcohol, unhealthy diet and certain medications such as antidepressants.[9] I've heard from women in their 60s and 70s who say that they find it difficult to meet sweethearts equipped to rumble in the bedroom. Yes, there's Viagra but it's expensive and not all men can take it.

Although most women think nothing of dating a man two or three years younger, some hesitate to go five, 10 or even 15 years younger. I dated someone five years younger when I was in my 30s and I remember making much ado about it. Since then, I've come to know women whose sweethearts are between 11 and 20 years younger and I now "get it!"

Older men are far more likely to be married than older women, which shrinks the dating pool.[10] In the U.S., life expectancy for women is five years more than it is for men, which further shrinks the dating pool for women over 50.[11] Add to this the fact that historically, men have readily coupled with younger, and even much younger, women. It simply makes sense to normalize mature women dating younger men. And you're mistaken if you conjure up the notion that there are no younger men who are interested in older women.

One + One >2

Once you commit to a dating site and have been active on it for a while, you'll become familiar with the "inventory" of men in your area and the average number of "connections" that you can expect on a weekly or monthly basis. After the first few weeks, the volume of "connections" will often pare down significantly and stabilize. This can be a good thing because it means that your profile, photos and filters are working.

Remember that filters work both ways. Men who are looking for a petite brunette who likes fishing, have probably filtered you out (unless you fit that description). You have likely filtered them out too in some way. So, you should be left with a waxing and waning short list of potential matches to "connect" with.

Online "connections" are facilitated by different sites in different ways. On Bumble, both you and the man have to right swipe each other before you can get in touch with each other.[12] On Match or eHarmony, many variations of outreach are offered, including sites that provide compatibility matches and encourage you to respond to a man who winks or messages you first. You can also wink or send a message proactively.

The bottom line is that you have to sort through the inventory and decide who and how many men to connect with. Balance quantity with sanity and self-care.

Over time, you'll get a sense for this connection funnel. If on average you get matched with four men per week who *seem* to meet some of your criteria, on closer inspection you'll see that only one probably comes close to fulfilling most of your criteria and he may not reach out to you. What do you do then? Treat this like a business. It sounds unromantic but it works. This is a numbers game and resilience is key!

If he doesn't reach out, then you reach out by commenting on some aspect of his profile; e.g., "Did you get to snorkel the Great Barrier Reef on your trip to Australia?" If he replies, you're off to the races with a light, responsive dialogue. Once you connect and engage with someone online, push to a phone meeting as fast as possible. Chapter 5 explains why.

If he doesn't reply, don't take it personally because you have no idea why he didn't reply. For all you know,

If he doesn't reply, don't take it personally because you have no idea why he didn't reply. Just move on.

his dog died. Just move on. Try another match — reach out if you feel there's enough potential with someone else or wait for more matches. You get the picture.

EXPERIMENT

Your profile and the filters that you select are fluid and can be changed anytime. Nothing is written in stone when you're using a dating site. Post, connect, meet and learn whether your profile is working the way you want it to. Then revise your profile as needed. To start, figure out what what's most important, implement filters that reflect your values, preferences and lifestyle. Then experiment.

It's like creating an abstract oil painting. You begin with a concept about color palette, size and approximate shape dimensions. Once you pick your canvas, opt for oil, acrylic or watercolor and work on the painting a bit, you might decide to tweak the palette or add more definition to the shapes. Similarly, you might get too many or too few connections on your dating site, or not the right kind at all. Go back, adjust your profile, swap out a photo or two or change the filters. Try again. This is a numbers game!

I grew up in the Pacific Northwest. When we were kids, my Mom made my siblings and me go hiking and biking, and swimming in cold Canadian lakes. She had us cross country skiing at age five. I continue to enjoy hiking, skiing and biking, and now I also do spinning and yoga to help keep me sane and manage my weight. Having an outdoor exercise partner is my ideal scenario. So, when I started dating, I posted that I wanted to meet someone who worked out at least five times a week.

What I found was that I connected with a mix of adrenalin junkies — a maniacal long-distance runner, and a hard-core triathlete who wasn't happy unless he was cresting a Colorado mountain or pushing through a 10-mile run in 95-degree weather with two German short-haired pointers at his side. He was obsessed with endurance exercising after losing what must have been 150 pounds, likely with the help of bariatric surgery. Both men were singularly focused on their competitions and nutrition. One was particularly eager to meet a size 2 lady who could outrun him. My full-figured body wasn't what either had in mind.

So, I re-evaluated my profile and dialed back the workout frequency; I changed it to wanting to meet someone who worked out two to three times a week, and this gave me many more suitable matches.

DEAL KILLERS

Let's move on to talk about deal killers. I made the decision to filter out men who were not legally divorced yet. Some people are well on their way to getting a divorce but are "technically" still married when they start to date. It's well known that men are more likely to remarry than women, and we all know about "casserole ladies" who attend to uncoupling men even before the wife has moved on.

I can see that there are plenty of understandable reasons to date before the decree is absolute — ranging from complex division of asset procedures, protracted custody battles and uncooperative spouses who stonewall divorce proceedings — but I neither wanted a front row seat to a combative domestic situation nor did I want to date someone who was just starting to find their dating legs. I figured that an almost-divorced guy would likely not be ready to embark on a serious, romantic journey.

In my mind, the worst-case scenario was that they'd be reviving a sex life that disappeared in the marriage three-plus years ago, and I would be a player in a sensuality rehab program. The best-case scenario was that they thought they were ready but not quite firing on all cylinders yet.

I felt strongly about drawing that line. That was just me. I may have been shooting myself in the foot but, still being married was a deal killer for me.

Also, I found that scammers commonly posted only one or two photos, and used the phrase, " … looking for a God-fearing woman," in their profile, so I put this line at the bottom of my profile:

If you are still legally married, don't have at least three photos posted or are looking for a "God-fearing woman," please pass me by.

If there are "deal killer" traits that you've filtered out but for some reason men who have those qualities are still responding to you online, then experiment by adding a phrase like this at the end of your profile:

If you are looking for a [fill in the blank] woman, please pass me by.

CHAPTER 3

SELECTING APPROPRIATE REPRESENTATIVE PHOTOS

How you present yourself matters. A lot. You will make your first impression with these photographs. They're critical because men are visual when it comes to dating. They tend to give in to what they're seeing and ask questions later.[13]

Invest in getting a professional photographer to take foundational, flattering photos of you with good lighting. Lots of women do this. Don't overthink it!

Invest in getting a professional photographer to take foundational, flattering photos of you with good lighting.

Even some high-resolution iPhone pictures taken by a talented, trusted friend will work. Then add a few candid lifestyle snapshots.

Like the face of Helen of Troy, let your smiling headshot be the picture that launches a thousand ships ... I mean online inquiries! Women appear most attractive to men when they're portraying happiness. Smiling can even compensate for beauty, relatively speaking, so post a gorgeous photo of your face — one that shows off your beautiful smile.[14]

Include at least one full body photo. Regardless of your proportions or body type, there is someone out there who is looking for you. Whether you are pear shaped, long and lean like a beanpole, or buxom and sturdy, there are men out there who think you're perfect. But pay attention to your appearance. Look your best by choosing clothes that flatter you.

Give viewers a strong sense of your favorite activities and lifestyle without necessarily spelling it all out in words. Post at least two or three lifestyle shots; e.g., swinging a golf club, speaking at an industry event or posing in front of the Golden Gate Bridge. Let these shots truly represent who you are and how you live. If your kitty is your best friend, put her in a photo to attract the cat lovers and deflect folks with cat allergies.

Selecting Appropriate Representative Photos

Show that you're a world traveller by sharing the photo of you under the Eiffel Tower.

It's also advisable to add your senior dad or children (whatever age), if they're a big part of your life and they're okay with that. It's also fine to leave them out. This is about you and your real-life story.

Recent and truly representative pictures of you are expected. Nothing speaks "ughhh" more than posting an old picture that looks nothing like you. When showing up for a first date, you'll notice the wind slowly whistle out of his sail when he sees you in person for the first time and you don't resemble your photo. If you're full-figured now but were 30 pounds slimmer 10 years ago, do not post the old picture. If you do, it conveys that you're neither realistic, happy nor confident with how you are now.

On that note, I also want to add that you do not need to lose those 30 pounds before you start your online dating journey. Experiment. You will see that there are men who like you just the way you are.

Refrain from flaunting a boudoir photo on a dating site. Although you may be proud to be buxom and you look ravishing in a merry widow, cheesecake photos in which you're provocatively dressed send an early message that sex is your currency. Yes, sensuality is a critical part of love and intimacy, but if a committed monogamous relationship is a priority for you, this takes you down the wrong digital road.

There are many wonderful, sensual men who would deeply appreciate that sexy photo if shared later, in private, once you've gotten to know and trust each other. You stand a good chance of those same men eliminating you as a potential lifetime partner candidate when they see that photo posted on a public forum like a dating site, even though they may connect with you and seem interested.

Avoid posting a picture with someone's arm around you, unless it's clear that that person is a family member. For some men, the smallest point of confusion will deflect them, even if it seems obvious that the other man is your father. Solo shots are best in my view; they invite the viewer to join you, at least in their mind.

Add photos with your children judiciously. If you have four kids and are looking for a midlife "eight is enough" situation, then show off a couple of photos with the happy clan playing touch football and "X" marks the spot where more kids could fit in. Otherwise, hold back if you're open to sharing the rest of your life with someone whose children don't play as large a role in his current life or who doesn't have children.

Avoid grainy photos. High-resolution photos are more credible, since scammers tend to use low-resolution photos that they've screen-scraped (See Chapter 5).

Don't post the entire roll of headshots just because they're all flattering. Limit photographs to about six. Remember, you can experiment by adding or deleting any photo any time if you want or if you change your mind.

CHAPTER 4

SCREENING CANDIDATES BY PHONE

PUSH TO THE PHONE

A heart that is looking for love again is a vulnerable heart, albeit a bold one. Before you reserve any part of your precious day to meet someone in person for the first time, push to talk by phone. Like dandelion blow ball seeds being strewn across a parking lot on a windy day, a multitude of dates may waste your time and dilute your hope for love, if you go on first dates without phone screening first. Eventually a string of mediocre or bad first-date experiences will accrue, and you'll become one of those women who emphatically declares that online dating doesn't work for her. And you'll be right. It didn't.

You will learn much about each other by phone screening. That's why employment recruiters rely

A heart that is looking for love again is a vulnerable heart, albeit a bold one.

heavily on phone interviews to save time. No matter how brief the first in-person date, you invest emotions like hope and anxiety, plus time — time thinking about the date, time getting dressed and time traveling to the destination. Shepherd your emotional energy and time with care by pushing to the phone first so that your heart and emotional energy stay "bright" for men who have a high potential of being a good fit for you.

Ask for his phone number and agree on a convenient time to speak. At this point, you need to temporarily take the lead to ensure that you transition from messaging online to talking, and also, to keep your phone number private. If he resists the phone call, a red flag should come up for you. Consider terminating the online exchanges and I recommend "blocking" him on the dating site if you cannot speak by phone.

Screening Candidates by Phone

Once the call is arranged, phone him and give this conversation your full attention. Confirm aspects of his profile by getting details. Don't multitask. If you sense that you don't have his full attention on the phone, ask what he's doing. This conversation should feel like a fun meet and greet, not like an inquisition, so tone of voice, how you frame questions and the levity and humor with which you speak are all important. At this stage in life, most of us are adept conversationalists when we need to be, and are reasonably skilled at diplomatically inquiring about anything that needs to be uncovered. At least it's not hard to tell when someone is avoiding a topic.

How a man speaks and the sound of his voice is a big deal. Most of us melt when we sense a witty or kind person on the other end. For me, a deep bass voice is icing on the cake. All the better if he's empathic and asks insightful questions. It's hard to connect when someone has an elevated or condescending inflection in his speech. A voice pitch that makes the hair on the back of your neck stand up, might be an unexpected deal breaker.

You should also assess whether he's able to balance leading the conversation with telling you about himself. Note whether he is listening to you and asking you relevant questions.

Some tips for this 30-minute phone conversation:

DO

- If he's been married, confirm that he's not still married by getting some details about his divorce or his wife's passing such as the date of death or his divorce attorney's name.

- Listen for and ask about anything that doesn't make sense; e.g., an accent that doesn't align with his story or surname, bad grammar even though his profile says he's well educated, etc.

- Uncover any commonalities like mutual friends, past places of work and so forth so that you can do some light online background checking (believe me, he's going to do the same for you).

DON'T

- Don't peddle the conversation for both of you. If there are awkward moments, silently take a long breath and wait to see if he fills them in.

- Refrain from introducing controversial topics especially politics and religion. Instead, stick to a kind, curious and fun inquiry and listen hard.

- Don't frontload this potential relationship by talking for more than about 30 minutes. If the conversation is going great, continue the momentum in person. You have the rest of your lives to share all your stories.

During the call, make an informed decision about whether there's enough of a fit to progress to a first date. If there isn't, clearly say so at the end of the phone call and move on.

No one likes rejection or rejecting. That's something all of us have in common. Let's tackle rejecting others here because I've heard that for some women, online dating feels uncomfortable because it requires weeding people out. Yup! It certainly does but curating goes both ways. They're weeding you out (or in), too.

No one likes rejection or rejecting. That's something all of us have in common.

Rejecting a potential suitor who seems to really like you is stressful especially for "empaths," yet neither giving up on trying to meet your sweetheart nor mercy dating serves anyone. Cutting losses is never easy but relatively speaking, when done on the phone at the beginning, it's *much* easier and much kinder. Later, when you've actually met in person and possibly kissed, rejection can burn and feel much more "personal." Plus, you will have invested more time and he's likely grown to like you even more, which makes it harder and more hurtful.

If he's the one who doesn't think that the two of you are a good fit and informs you by phone, be grateful and move on. Don't take it personally. He saved you heartache later.

Move on to an in-person date if the phone conversation is a success. Let him ask you out and be ready to make it easy by having a couple of date and time options that work for you in your back pocket.

When I first connected with Johannes, we were both energized by how much we had in common. He had multiple businesses, traveled for fun and did a lot of outdoor sports. There seemed to be tremendous chemistry on the phone. We laughed and laughed as we volleyed questions back and forth but then I noticed that he made a few references to his church, too.

So, I started listening to discern whether he was looking for a devout Christian woman. Johannes was relatively new to online dating and hadn't referenced religion in his profile. The more we gently discussed his lifestyle, the more obvious it became that ideally, he and his future sweetheart would practice his faith together. I suspected that this wouldn't be me. I'm spiritual but it's more along the lines of *namaste*.

It was Johannes who actually took the plunge, rejecting me by leaving me a voice mail message afterwards.

You excite and energize me a lot! Too much actually. I have a very dynamic, active life and find that for me, I need a woman who is the opposite of me — someone who calms me down. And also someone who shares my faith. I don't think that we're the fit that we're both looking for. You have a lot to offer and I wish you all the best!

So, Johannes fell off the table as a prospective sweetheart before we even met, but that was a good thing. I was truly grateful to him for not wasting our time. We both got back the opportunity to focus on qualifying and setting up phone dates with others who were better aligned. And I respected him for leading us to this temporarily uncomfortable but right outcome.

LIMIT TEXTING

Don't substitute the first phone conversation or in-person meeting with a texting dialogue. You will probably not get the breadth of insights that you should have. This is especially true if you don't want to waste time with married men, since the internet is becoming a very common form of infidelity.[15]

In fact, generally stay away from texting except to receive and reciprocate "small chirps" as signs of life and ongoing interest; e.g., "TGIF! Hope you arrived home safely from Chicago." By its very nature, texting creates unreasonable urgency. Texting protocol is fraught with ambiguity and texting chemistry is no assurance of actual chemistry.

It's confounding how many women say that they've met the right guy or that they've even got a relationship going before they've spoken or met him, all based on texting.

And men seem to love the repartee and anonymity of digital flirtation. These protracted text chats run a higher risk of bonding with someone who is not the person you think he is because:

- in person he's shy, not the extraverted, sexy persona that you experience online;
- he's 10+ years older than his online photos; or
- he's married or a scammer.

Intense texting had been going on with Claire and Mike for over a week. They were instantly tethered after connecting online, toggling back and forth daily, flirting, joking, comparing favorite vacation destinations and much more. Finally, their first date came and Claire was excited. She bought a new outfit, had her car washed and made sure that she knew the route to the wine bar where they were going to meet.

Mike never showed up. He did call her, feigning confusion saying that he was at another location — a bar by the same name — but he made no effort to come over to where she was. Ten bucks says that he was married and had done this before for a digital thrill. Needless to say, Claire was less enthusiastic about online dating after this.

A pre-date phone call might have provided a better sense of who he was and whether he was still married. In summary, push to the phone, minimize texting and then push to the in-person first date.

CHAPTER 5

DEALING WITH SCAMMERS AND JERKS

SCAMMERS

Scammers exist and will likely target you at some point, especially when you first join a dating site. I know this feels intimidating, but don't let that stop you.

Scammers are unable to meet in person in my experience. They are either conveniently out of state or can't get together at any near future time, typically using a business or family-related type of excuse such as a work trip or sick child. Be very wary when there isn't a mutually convenient time to meet in a public place in the near future — I'd say within the next 10 days or so. Skip them and move on.

One + One >2

Scammers will likely target you at some point. I know this feels intimidating, but don't let that stop you.

The first three men who messaged me when I first joined Match were hands down the most attractive men I'd come across on the site and seemed the most desirable of the short list of prospects that I'd compiled. One was an attorney in a tuxedo; another was a fit, handsome father with a boy on his shoulders. The third was a rugged architect whose headshot showed him in Oakley sunglasses driving his SUV. They were also the ones who reached out to me the fastest, each with sweet, long messages demonstrating that they'd read my profile and were sincerely interested in me. None of them had posted more than three photos. One man only posted one picture and most of the pictures were low resolution.

With the first man, I volleyed messages a few times. I started to notice grammar mistakes that seemed out of character for an attorney. I had indicated on my

Dealing with Scammers and Jerks

---

profile that I was looking to meet someone local yet he was from Florida. So I pushed to the phone, making it clear that I was done with online chats. Wouldn't you know — he had a strong foreign accent that didn't make sense given his online profile and Anglo name. I asked more and more questions and was careful not to give information about myself. He was coy and of course he couldn't meet me.

"Sorry but I don't think this is going to work out," I told him on the phone after hearing the accent. I reported him as a scammer on Match and blocked him on my cell phone.

This happened again with the next man who messaged me a long-winded note asking,

"How did you sleep, angel?" This guy was not only a widower but he had recently lost both parents in a car accident. He was out of town for work so he couldn't meet me either. When I asked where he was and what he was doing, he wove an intricate story about being in Seattle bidding on a design contract to build an orphanage in Indonesia.

"Amazing," I commented. "That must be a well-endowed, nonprofit! I don't think this is going to work out," I said again, reporting him to Match and blocking his number. This was over a span of about two or three days.

Since I'm a widow and indicated that on my Match profile, I noticed that the scammers were all alleged widowers, too. Our tragedies mirrored each other's but theirs always included an additional tragedy. It seemed that they were trying to hotwire an emotional connection not only by virtue of our shared widowhood but also by playing on my heartstrings with an egregious additional loss. In each case, they had either recently lost parents in a car accident or had a sick child pass away.

After the initial two "scam" connections, I was like a spider waiting for the fly. When I told the third man, a handsome "widower" in San Diego, that I was going to call him, he suddenly messaged me to let me know in advance that he had an accent. I immediately called him, and said, "Busted!" I hung up, sent another report to Match and blocked his number.

I quickly shared these experiences with girlfriends and subsequently even with my first in-person date with an oil engineer. They told me stories about other women who'd experienced similar situations. The men that these women had connected with were never local and could never meet in-person. Despite this, the women kept interacting with them online. Eventually, each man asked for money on the pretense of needing it to help a sick child or to travel to meet the woman. One woman declared bankruptcy over the money that she'd given the guy she was messaging and texting with.

After I noticed these common attributes among the scammers, I became cautious in any of these circumstances:

- He appeared handsome and age appropriate but posted no more than three photos on his profile;
- His photos were grainy;
- He messaged me a "story" that mirrored my profile in some way but his story "trumped" mine;
- His profile indicated that he was looking for a "God-fearing woman"; or
- When we spoke on the phone, he had an accent that didn't correlate to his surname or background.

I always terminated an online connection immediately if any **one** of these attributes were present:

- His first outreach to me was a presumptive and overly sweet long message;

- He could not meet me in person, locally, within two weeks of speaking by phone; or
- I noticed a lot of bad grammar or misspelled commonly used words, despite professing to be educated on his profile.

The good news is that all of my encounters with scammers happened at the outset of my online dating journey and within five days, one after the other. I became good at spotting them and honestly, after the first week they stopped.

Lastly, if someone hints at a need for or asks you for money, terminate and block the connection immediately. They won't ask you for money on the first communication, however, and probably not even on the second or fourth message. These men are con artists, teasing you along until they've garnered trust and affection from you.

Push all good prospects to the phone. Then push to an early in-person meeting.

JERKS

A jerk of some sort will probably cross your dating path at some point despite careful phone screening. It happened to me on my second dating cycle and when it did, it really took my breath away and made me take a break — a teeny, tiny one.

Andy, a 50-something father of four and a long, lean tennis player, was Swiss-like in his punctuality (not one of my virtues). He was also vitriolic and rude. Admittedly, I showed up 10 minutes late to our first meeting, not showing up as my "best self" that day but I'd texted him en route to let him know.

When I arrived at the bistro, Andy was already drinking a beer. Red flags started flapping in my head when he smugly suggested that I get myself a drink at the bar. I wondered whether my lateness was a mortal sin or whether previous tardy dates had turned out really badly for him. Pulling myself together, I smiled, sat down with a glass of wine and tried to right whatever wrong was at hand. I'd come this far so I might as well "learn" what was going on with him, right?

It got worse. He pushed an iPad towards me asking me to show him on Google Maps where my hometown was. I pointed to it nervously. He carried on like this spewing out questions about geography and education. My blood started to bubble like tar on a West Texas highway but I managed to slip in a few questions about his marriage and children before he finished his

One + One >2

---

beer, got up and left for a tennis game that he'd warned me about when I arrived.

What a jerk! I never saw or spoke to him again. It took me a few days to recompose myself and to this day, I have no idea why he acted the way he did. Given the odd geography interrogation with his iPad, I bet that my tardiness was not the only thing that had set him off. I dusted his toxic energy off me, blocked his phone number and online profile, and moved on.

To put this in perspective, it happened with one out of the 16 men that I met in person by then. Those are reasonable odds, don't you think? Hopefully you won't encounter a jerk but if you do, consider it an occupational hazard. Hang in there. "Block" him and move on. This is a numbers game.

Hopefully you won't encounter a hater but if you do, consider it an occupational hazard. Hang in there. "Block" him and move on.

CHAPTER 6

TARGET: MEETING EIGHT MEN IN PERSON

Chances are you're not going to meet that right-fit man right out of the gate just because you clicked your red heels like Dorothy and went online. Dating is a journey. It doesn't have to be a marathon but it's probably not a sprint. The journey can be rich and filled with self-discovery, inspiration and fun, though.

So, how many men do you have to meet along this journey before Prince Charming enters stage right and you end up in an exclusive relationship that could evolve into marriage? There's no hard and fast rule but since I love statistics and probability, I figured that I'd

One + One >2

*Dating is a journey.
It doesn't have to be a marathon
but it's probably not a sprint.*

---

borrow the venture capital framework, which espouses the rule of "10." If you invest in 10 companies, at least one will hit a home run. So, I made "10" my target goal. This meant that if I dated 10 eligible men, then I expected one of them to be a right-fit. I kept track in a spreadsheet in case I had to go on more than one dating journey.

"Eligible" meant that I had phone-screened them before meeting in person and they seemed ready for a committed relationship. "Dated" meant that I had met them in person at least two to three times. It did not mean that we'd slept together.

What I found was that it actually took me "dating" eight men in each dating cycle. I ended up in two dating cycles over the course of three and a half years. A "dating cycle" was officially over for me once I was in an exclusive relationship for one year. This meant that

I'd been asked and agreed to be in an exclusive relationship, we each contacted anyone else we were dating to end those affiliations, we'd both deactivated our online dating accounts, and we'd experienced one year together in an exclusive, great-fit relationship.

In each of my two dating cycles, it took about four months for me to meet someone who seemed like a great fit. Funnily enough, four months was about all I could do anyway, because a dating traffic jam would build up.

The multitude of prospects and dates that wove in and out of my life over the course of a few months would build and start to get complicated. Due to scheduling conflicts, I'd go on a second date with a promising prospect one month after meeting him. In the meantime, two other interested prospects connected with me and I'd go on first dates with each of them right away. So, during some weeks, it felt as if I was dating three people, yet the preceding two or three weeks, it had been silent at the O.K. Corral with the same old inventory on the dating site.

About half of the men that I dated, only dated one woman at a time. Some had a moral conviction around it simply being the "right" thing to do while others frankly admitted that dating more than one woman at a time was much too confusing. They wouldn't be able to keep their names straight. The other 50 percent that I dated were definitely dating other women at the same time as me. How do I know? We talked about it if it came up but usually I didn't need verbal confirmation. I had strong intuition around it.

Stick-handling conversations about whether either one of us was dating other people at the same time, was truly an art. Whenever the subject came up, I did disclose what I was up to and why, explaining in a straightforward way that I was also seeing other men and would continue to do so until I met and agreed to be in an exclusive relationship. I made it clear that the "exclusive relationship" was my goal. If the question never came up, I neither asked about nor "told" on the first two dates.

I have to say that it got a little hairy sometimes, though. Once, I made the embarrassing mistake of texting John, "Thank you for dinner," referencing his daughter by the name of another man's daughter. Not my best moment!

Dating more than one person in the early stage serves a few purposes. It definitely saves time. Tick, tock. As we mature we become only too aware of how fleeting time can be. There's an art to striking a balance between savoring time and wasting it.

Apply the carpe diem philosophy to the dating realm to embrace all high potential opportunities when they cross your path, not later. If three opportunities present simultaneously, then take them all. Make it a priority just like you would if you were pursuing a dream job. If three good interview invitations came your way in the same week, you would figure out a way to take them all.

As an over-thinker, I typically need to check out all the shoe stores in a mall to validate how I feel about the pair that I end up buying…the ones I probably spotted in the first or second store. As much as I am loathe to compare shoe shopping with dating men, I'm doing it to make make the point that dating two or more men contemporaneously can be extremely effective in helping gauge how you "really" feel when you are with them, not how you "think" you feel.

Contemporaneous dating also prevents you from overinvesting emotionally in any one relationship that seemed great online but is in fact only decent in person. My goal was to feel "great" when I was with him. There were several men whose online profiles seemed wonderful — they were accomplished, attractive, divorced or widowed. In person, they were considerate, generous and honest, but I only felt "okay" with them, not "great." We talked but I was the one who had to come up with all the topics. They were handsome but after three dates we still had no chemistry. You get the picture. Could we have gotten into a committed relationship and worked through it? Who knows?

This brings me back to shoe shopping. Every now and then there would be a man who, on paper, had some of the attributes that I wanted but not most of them. In person he was exceptionally funny, resourceful, imaginative, charming or thoughtful, though. He had a "je ne sais quoi," that cinched me. It wasn't quite chemistry. It was a combination of quality with a strong potential for chemistry. When it was subtle at the beginning, I was able to recognize it better by comparing how I felt when I was dating other men around the same time.

Some busy women meet two or three men in a day. I'd end up emotionally overwhelmed if I did that so I tended to avoid this. While there's nothing morally wrong with meeting or dating more than one man when you're not in a committed relationship, some of you will not feel comfortable doing that, and that's fine. Just know where you stand and why.

CHAPTER 7

PRACTICE THE THREE-DATE RULE

You may never get a sense of a Russian River cabernet sauvignon's complexity until you take the time to decant it first. Similarly, the love of the second half of your life might be understated, preferring not to enchant you at the first encounter but rather opting to sweep you off your feet over time, like a fine old-vine wrapping itself around you gradually. Or, he simply might need time to trust and learn you before fully revealing himself.

Some people are lucky enough to fall in love at first sight and then stay together for a lifetime. Though juicy and intoxicating, my "fell in love at first sight" relationships didn't last. They were usually fatally flawed and didn't survive the test of time. Now, I need

Though juicy and intoxicating, my "fell in love at first sight" relationships didn't last. They were usually fatally flawed and didn't survive the test of time.

a slow burn when falling in love. It makes me feel as if we've earned the spectacular series of vistas that grace our horizon as we push up a hill together. I trust this dynamic more.

The three-date rule means that once you commit to a first date with someone, you secretly commit to dating him three times in total. This presumes that he asks you out again or that you don't uncover any deal breaker such as dog allergies or deceit, etc.

With Thomas, the three-date rule really worked for me. We had had a truly "mediocre" series of initial dates. The first time, I met him for a glass of wine at an uptown, over-50 restaurant that had seen its heyday in the '90s. When I arrived, the parking lot was full. I'd forgotten cash for the valet so I spent too much time circling, looking for a spot. I hated my outfit — a pair of black slacks, a white T-shirt with a perfunctory black and white striped cardigan, nothing feminine or particularly flattering. What was I thinking?

Like a congressman in a navy jacket with gold buttons, he was standing, waiting for me at the bar. Thomas had grey — almost white — short hair, sharp blue eyes and spoke with an uncommonly Southern twang. He made overly grand gestures pulling the bar chair out for me and insisting on a 9-ounce pour of wine.

Wrong choice! I thought. I was definitely going to have wine, but a 9-ounce pour seemed irresponsible since I was driving myself home. He awkwardly grappled with conversational topics, I was hungry, and we both became a bit annoyed; we stumbled through the date.

Thomas walked me to my car and, to my surprise, asked to see me again. At the time, I was also dating (and favoring) a tall NASA mathematician with a penchant for Italian race cars. Plus, I was heading home to Canada for the holidays and then on to Lake Tahoe to ski with girlfriends. The whole trip would last one month.

Christmas came and went. Just as the plane's wheels touched down in Houston on January 3, five weeks after the first date, I received a brief text from Thomas:

One + One >2

"Welcome back to Houston."

It was a small gesture but exquisitely timed. Since I'd made that three-date commitment to myself, we went out on two more dates. The second date wasn't much better than the first. His hair was meticulously combed, he was freshly showered and there were more grand gestures — car doors being opened in a sweeping way — but then he did a bait and switch on me. He suddenly asked me to forgo the movie we'd agreed to see, so we could meet up with a fishing buddy of his who was in town for one night.

It occurred to me that this bait and switch maneuver was his deliberate attempt to test my emotional elasticity and he later confirmed this. Although perturbed, I agreed because I was curious about how far he would take this type of "switching" behavior, plus I wanted to see what his friends were like. The movie could wait.

We went to a British pub and ate greasy fish and fries. The music was loud. His whiskered friend was jovial but seemed like a redneck from the coast. There were four or five other friends and they were very pleasant. Overall, I wasn't overly impressed and there was no chemistry, but I had a nice time.

By the time the third date rolled around on a Wednesday, I realized that I had double booked myself with the NASA mathematician. I called Thomas apologetically but resolute about rescheduling our date to Thursday. Instinctively he figured out what had happened and surprised me by saying,

"I'd really looked forward to seeing you tonight but all right, I'll take your Thursday ... AND your Saturday, too, then."

Saturday was Valentine's Day. Very strategic and bold! Something had suddenly ignited in Thomas. It might have been the cut and thrust of knowing that there was competition, although I'd like to think that it was because he had gotten to know me better. In the end, it didn't matter. What I do know is that he suddenly upped his game sprinkling a hefty load of romance into those dates — bringing flowers, making witty comments, and massaging my feet under the table on the fourth date! He managed to slide us into an exclusive, committed relationship for well over a year.

Although our cultural differences ignited some exciting combustible chemistry in our relationship, in the end that same cultural divide was too wide to bridge. By mutual choice, the relationship did not lead to a lifetime commitment, but I firmly stand by the three-date rule.

    I got to pressure test that rule again in the following dating cycle. Like fine wine that needs time to breathe before revealing its full character, the qualities that you are looking for in your potential sweetheart may surface on the second, third or even fourth date.

CHAPTER 8

NAVIGATING FIRST DATES

MINDSET

Mindset is the key to experiencing dating as a joyful process. Meeting for the first time can be draining. You've invested time into prequalifying each other, you're anxious about what he really looks like, whether he will like you, and you're wondering whether there will be chemistry. There's also a modicum of stress if you're showing up at a venue you've never been to before: how should you dress, how do you get there, where will you park, etc.

Pay careful attention to your mindset taking care to manage your moods and any anxiety. Practice the art of being someone who is fun to spend time with. Even if the two of you are not a "fit," you're still doing something you like such as sipping lattes in a favorite café or getting in a walk by the river. You'll become wiser, sexier and more magnetic with the confidence and unique insights about men that you get from dating at this stage of your life.

Be your best self every time. Dress with verve. Get the lipstick and scarves out. Have your nails done. Wear something feminine but don't overdress. For fresh ideas, check out Pinterest boards such as, "Outfits for Women Over 50," "Aging Gracefully" and more.

Enjoy yourself. Receive compliments graciously, express delight and savor the fun.

Let yourself be courted. Just in case there's a twitch deep inside of you that feels as if you "owe" him something because he bought you a glass of wine, banish the thought and never think of it again. The man is supposed to pay for the first date — whether coffee or a meal. He wants to please and provide for you, and your job is to "be pleased." You don't "owe" him anything beyond courtesy and respect at this point.

Don't "hotwire" a relationship by jumping into "girlfriend" or "wife" mode. The goal on the first date is get to know each other better; therefore, don't offer to help organize his kitchen, meet and cook for his children or plan his birthday dinner for 20 friends the next weekend. *Be still.* Get to that second date, *the diva dinner date.* Learn him so that you can make an informed and confident decision about whether you'd ever consider becoming his girlfriend if he broaches the subject down the road.

SAFETY

Always meet in a public place and get there on your own steam on a first date; for example, drive your own car. Use common sense about safety regardless of how well you feel you already know him from a phone chat or electronic exchanges. Consider giving his name and phone number to a close friend or family member and text them within the first hour to confirm that you're okay.

I've also heard that some ladies have a friend call them to check in. One man I dated even offered to show me his driver's license to help validate that he was who he said he was.

MORE TIPS

No alcoholic beverages beforehand. Arrive confident, calm, on time and firing on all faculties, not with the liquid courage of vodka.

Go slow. Like you, he might be unsure how the process works if he hasn't dated in a decade or two, or if he's been dating exclusively for a while. Give yourselves a chance to take each other in. At this life phase, jumping into things can have disastrous consequences, so take your time. Don't rush any aspect of the first encounter.

Conversation Starters. Intentionally leave conversation gaps especially at the beginning, to see how outgoing and socially adept he is. See what kind of tone he sets and where he wants to take the conversation. Admittedly, women are usually better at this unless your date is in sales, but give it a few minutes to see where he takes things.

If light banter isn't getting off the ground because he's shy, anxious or just not good at kicking off dialogue, then go ahead and jump in with some neutral inquiries like:

- Have you lived here long?
- Where did you grow up?
- If you had the opportunity to go on a road trip next month, where would you go?
- Are you taking any vacations this summer (winter)?

You can offer open-ended questions like these if more dialogue prodding is needed later on:

- Tell me about your family.
- If money was no object, where would you live?
- How do you see yourself spending most of your time in five (or ten) years?
- How do you typically spend your birthdays?

Listen hard and well. Show that you've read his profile by asking specific questions about him, and then listen intently. Notice if he runs on in conversation like a wild horse let out of a confined paddock, telling you more in an hour than some will in their lifetime. Is he curious about you, volleying questions your way as well? This is exactly what you should be eager to experience for better or for worse. It's all part of getting to know each other so that you can later decide if you'd like to be in an exclusive relationship.

Avoid negativity. Refrain from political rants and mentioning how bad your week was or how much your work environment annoys you. It ruins the mood and leads to the conclusion that there's drama in your life. Try not to discuss exes — former boyfriends or husbands — but answer questions if asked. If you're widowed, it's perfectly fine to reference your late spouse.

Don't overstay. I can't say that there's a guideline as to whether 40 or 70 minutes is enough for a coffee or glass of wine meeting, but I'd venture to say that three hours is too much. Even if you feel intoxicated by each other on the first date — you really hit it off, have a million things in common, can't stop talking and feel as if you've known each other in another lifetime — don't let your glass of wine morph into a full-blown steak dinner. You run the risk of "fun fatigue."

If this is the "real thing" for you — awesome! Pat yourself on the back for all of the pre-work that you did: subscribing, posting, researching, talking on the phone and "showing up" when others might never even gotten to the point where they pull out their credit card for an online dating subscription. You're not over the finish line yet, though. You're not even close.

Let him take the lead to get you to the second date. Don't be coy, but don't force the conversation around your calendar when he hasn't even made up his mind how to handle the next step. And don't ask for feedback on how he thinks the date is going. He may not ask you out again right away but in my experience, men who are interested quickly signal that they want to continue spending time together and ask about availability at the end of the first date or the next day.

Go home alone. Really! You don't know each other yet. You might think that you do after a flirt-a-thon or tell-all first date, but you don't. Even if you feel unbelievably safe and comfortable with him, like he's "the one," or you haven't had sex in "way too long" — don't do it! You'd be denying yourself the romantic dating phase of your potential "forever" relationship.

The dating phase is a delicious mental nectar that will nourish the romantic artery of your relationship for the rest of your lives together. Enjoy it. There's no need to hurry.

I've heard complaints from women whose boyfriends don't take them out to dinner. They say that their boyfriends just want to "Netflix and chill." The women lament that they possibly fell into bed with these men…drum roll… too early…on the first date. As grown-ups, there's nothing morally wrong with sex on the first date. It might even seem natural for many given our current, on-demand culture but I personally think it makes uncoupling harder later if you end up not being a great fit for other reasons. When there's great chemistry and sex right out of the gate, you often end up biased towards the relationship, shoe-horning yourself into it more than you would have if you'd waited to learn about each other more first. Don't jumpstart things.

Don't hold it against him if he tries to bed you on the first date. Decline but receive it as a compliment! If he makes a play to take the first date between the sheets, then chances are that he's smitten with you and feeling ignited. He's also a risk-taker with an admirable level of testosterone.

It's not always easy for midlife men to muster the bravado to inveigle a confident lady into bed right away. After all, most have emerged from dramatic life circumstances themselves — financial challenges after divorce or becoming widowed, the onset of age-related limitations including hearing loss and sexual impotency and much more. For good reason, many men have doubts about whether their apparatus will even rise to the occasion when it's supposed to. So, honor his brazenness and spirit. You're mature enough to wholly *receive* and *own* that swaggering gesture.

Navigating First Dates

Raul pointedly made brazen advances in the parking lot as he walked me to my car on our first date. We'd been laughing our way through a couple of glasses of Tannat and a cheese plate. When I told him that it was time for me to go, he made it clear that he wanted us to sleep together that night. He had distinguished salt and pepper hair, tight strong thighs and a Porsche waiting to whisk us off. I admired the bravado that reared its stallion head but was also resolute in resisting:

"I'm flattered, but no thanks. I'm sure it would be wonderful, but so far I like you too much and want to get to know you better first."

Text within 12 to 24 hours of the first date, briefly thanking him and giving at least one compliment to demonstrate that you paid attention; e.g., "I hope that your daughter, Megan, has a wonderful birthday this weekend."

GHOSTING

If he didn't clearly state that he'd like to see you again somewhere along the line on the first date, and he hasn't texted or called you within 48 hours of the first date, move on. You've probably been "ghosted."

Just register that and move on to other prospects after checking his box on your spreadsheet.

Expect to get ghosted at some point and don't take it personally when it happens. Dating is not a popularity contest. You probably have no idea what's really going on with him and it's better not to guess. Again, his dog might have died the day following your date. It could have nothing to do with you. Dating is like falling when you're skiing; if you don't fall at least once, then you're not taking enough chances.

John, an even-featured, buff financial advisor who was also a racing cyclist, took me out twice — once for a "meet and greet" coffee date and then for the diva dinner date. He mentioned that he was also dating another woman. Feeling sheepish and a bit guilty, he said that he wanted me to know that because he planned on kissing me after dinner. He'd just gotten

Expect to get ghosted at some point so don't take it personally when it happens.

divorced after a 15-year marriage and wasn't sure what the dating protocol was in a situation like this. We got along well and seemed mutually attracted to each other. I was dating others, too.

That's fair, I thought. Indeed, he kissed me on my dark porch that night, a perfect end to a romantic evening.

Later that week, he told me that he was going on a much-needed vacation to the Texas Hill Country with bikes and some buddies, so he'd be incommunicado for four days. After that, I heard nothing for over a week. I texted twice, briefly, to see if John was okay, but got no response. I then left him alone, realizing that I had been "ghosted" and, yes, it felt weird and wrong for a while, but in the big scheme of life it wasn't a big deal. Other things must have been going on with him, but I had no way of knowing what they were.

Although we only had two dates and not three, I checked the box for John on my spreadsheet — he was number six — and moved on to the next prospects. Oddly enough, John texted me out of the blue four months later. I never replied. The momentum was lost and I was already in a new relationship. He was a good person. I silently wished him good fortune but blocked his number on my phone.

One + One >2

How you handle these situations is your call, but the important thing is not to agonize over the reasons why someone ghosts you. Don't be that person who can't let go or who has to know "why." You often have no way of knowing. It's more important to keep your dating momentum moving forward.

CHAPTER 9

SECOND DATE DIVA DINNER

Let's assume that you've been asked out on that second date. Usually this is a dinner date out and it's your night to relax and shine! He wants to see if he can "please" you. C'mon! Wear a dress. Add a scarf, lipstick and a gorgeous handbag. Be a svelte diva, a gorgeous phoenix or a sultry siren, but be ready to have him squire you around town. Your job is to be spoiled and to show that you're enjoying it, if that's true for you. At least have fun.

It's okay to drive yourself to dinner and meet him at the restaurant if you're still concerned about privacy or safety, but know that most men will offer to pick you up at your home. After all, they want to learn about you, too — see where you live and confirm that you live alone, if that's the case. If you're comfortable with that, be ready to leave when he arrives. If it makes sense,

One + One >2

---

introduce him to any adult family members or friends that live with you but skip the home tour — save that for another day. Remember, *go slow*.

Let him take the lead. You are still in "learning him" mode, so sit back. Pay attention to everything and engage with joy. Read between the lines, noting what his choices and manners tell you about him. How do you feel about the venue he selected? Is he organized or a "wing it" kind of guy? Does he open doors for you naturally or just because you're in a dress and on a date? Is he looking at you or his phone? How does he treat the wait staff?

Let him pick up the check … again. Yup! Pressure test his willingness to please you. Remember that he selected the venue so he had some control over the expense. Don't spring for half. You can make it up to him by treating him to dinner or a special event the

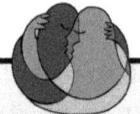

Let him take the lead.
You are still in "learning him" mode, so sit back.
Pay attention to everything and engage with joy.

Second Date Diva Dinner

next time. For now, you're being courted. This is also a good opportunity to gauge his financial elasticity.

Enjoy your alcoholic beverages but keep your faculties sharp and your discernment steady. Watch to see how much he drinks. Worst-case scenario is that the two of you finish a bottle of wine. Six vodka tonics are probably not okay. Use a ride share service to get home as needed.

A friend of mine used to deliberately schedule dinner dates on Sundays. She felt it gave her better insight into a potential drinking problem since overindulging on a Saturday is not that out of the ordinary. On Sunday night, however, most of us would refrain from tying one on if work or volunteer responsibilities were looming over us Monday morning.

Touch his arm lightly or brush your knee up against his at some point if there haven't been any affectionate gestures so far because this time, you may want to help tee up a kiss after dinner. It's not mandatory but I'll foreshadow the fact that if he hasn't kissed you by the third date, you may be "friend zoning" each other.

As before, don't sleep with him yet. Continue to pressure test his willingness to please you by waiting. In summary, the same tips that applied for the first date, apply for the second except that this time, there's

*Don't sleep with him yet.
Continue to pressure test his willingness
to please you by waiting.*

no need to leave early. Your night on the town should be effervescent and relaxed, so enjoy a long, luscious dinner.

CHAPTER 10

THE THIRD DATE

YOU'RE THE HOST

Now it's your turn to host, assuming that your date let you know that he'd like to continue seeing you. I recommend planning a memorable, fun activity within your budget. Make it one that not only reciprocates his generosity but also shows off your talents, whether it's your knowledge of local gems like a favorite, hidden wing in the museum of fine arts or a creative, unusual activity. Make sure you plan the details well by checking the weather, reserving a romantic quiet table, figuring out parking in advance or being ready to order a ride-share service.

Tell him beforehand and again at the outset, to refrain from pulling out his wallet. By making it clear up front that you're "inviting" him, you're demonstrating that you can take care of him, too. This is a deeply valued quality in midlife as we each search for a trusted partner to embark on the aging journey with. At some point, each of us needs to know who we can rely on if we get sick or injured. We'd all like to believe that that person is our sweetheart. So, invite him to relax and experience your hospitality and capacity to take care of things too, including the bill.

You're still in learning mode, and this date is critical because at the end of it, you should have a sense of whether you'd make a good couple. So, as you show him a great time, pressure test his flexibility a bit. A fair amount of elasticity is a necessary ingredient as you adapt to each other's value sets, passions, hobbies, first families, personalities (whether introvert or extrovert) and much more.

By midlife, some people have severely constricted their views and curtailed their willingness to try new things. For you, this could be a deal killer. It was for me. So, it's important to experience each other's aptitudes for trying out new situations and adapting.

However, I don't recommend anything too controversial. If you're not sure what his stance on gun control is or the impact of gunshots on his hearing, taking him to the shooting range to practice target shooting could be the wrong move.

My "go-to" third date always involved bike riding on one-speed cruisers followed by a casual dinner. I deliberately set out to confirm that my dates really could get on a bike comfortably and enjoy being surprised by me (I didn't tell them exactly where we were going at the outset) but I also made an effort to demonstrate thoughtfulness and caring by planning something tailored to their interests. I live in a neighborhood with long bike paths along the bayou, a lot of community events and whimsical cocktail lounges. I rode an old orange Schwinn and had a red men's cruiser from Walmart plus an extra helmet, ready for my date.

Sometimes we cycled along a bike path to the Sixth Ward of Houston, a lesser-known but charming historic neighborhood about 25 minutes away by bike. I'd take them on a brief tour showing them the welding shop of a local art car artist, an 1881 cottage that I'd renovated, and a cluster of run-down Victorian homes rumored to be the offices of a private eye who specializes in murder cases. Then I'd take them to the Iron Horse dive bar for a cold beer before dinner.

Other times we cycled to community-style opera in a local converted church by my home after an early dinner. Once I gave a tour of three whiskey watering holes that each had unique food trucks and live music.

There was never a time when my date didn't have a huge grin on his face at the end of the night, and a few men told me that it was the best date that they'd ever been on.

As you plan a date like this, keep in mind there's no pass/fail framework. Dating is the sandbox within which you learn about each other.

Funnily enough, the two men that I ended up in relationships with both objected to my nighttime bike ride dates for odd reasons. They wouldn't do it. Later, we ended up cycling a lot, even at night and on roads much more dangerous than those in my little neighborhood. My point is that my dates with them didn't "fail" because they refused to cycle at night with me, but I did make a mental note of how they needed to be in control, and wondered whether I might be okay with that.

As you plan this date, keep in mind there's no pass/fail framework. Dating is the sandbox within which you learn about each other.

"GO/NO-GO" DECISION

My experience was that decisions are normally made about dating each other exclusively on the third date. It just organically happens that way — that magical number three again. If he isn't a good fit, you'll typically know it by the end of this date and you simply shouldn't, in good conscience, lead him on if you feel that's it clear to you.

And if you haven't been kissed by the end of the third date, "Houston, you have a problem!" Something is not working. You may never know why but it probably doesn't matter. It's not working.

If by chance you're confused about whether you like your date enough to consider an exclusive relationship, force yourself to figuratively *stand up and shoot* by asking yourself who you'd rather be with. If someone else comes to mind or if you'd rather be alone, then it's not working. There's no need for you to dissect it and unpack it verbally with him, but you do have to make a go/no-go decision.

Occasionally, on a third date, the voice in my head was flummoxed, a whisper that I resisted when I should have made a "no-go" decision.

But he's an architect, he loves to cook and we both love classic movies..., I told myself about the blue-eyed architect, whose long bar tab for 13 Bulleit bourbons somehow landed on my credit card! This vexing dating scenario lumbered along for a few months before I finally cut the tether. At the end of our third date, I had what I needed to know about whether there was an incompatibility. I chose to ignore it. The bottom line is that at the end of the third date, you will probably know if there's a problem — although you may not know what it is — and you should graciously end it. No mercy dating!

But if you are really into each other, then there's one more step before deciding whether to date exclusively: sex. More on that shortly.

UNCOUPLING

"Uncoupling" means that one of you "leads" an uncomfortable conversation about not dating each other anymore so that you can both move on to meet your "right-fit" sweethearts. If you lead the conversation, he will usually want to know why you're rejecting him. Be kind. Let him go the way you found him — hopeful. Blame it on chemistry or the fact that you realize that you might not be as ready for someone with five children as you'd hoped you'd be.

In my experience, the right moment to have the uncoupling conversation is on the third date, or shortly thereafter, and it usually presents itself organically. I always wanted to be as kind, yet honest, as possible, so I organized my thoughts beforehand. I generally said something like this:

> *Adam, I've really enjoyed getting to know you over these last few weeks. You are an amazing man with a great sense of humor [or, fill in the blank with a true, specific compliment], and you're a wonderful catch for the right-fit lady you're looking for.*
>
> *However, I want to be honest and say that I don't think we're "the match" that you and I are both looking for. But I'm glad I got to spend time with you.*

Whatever you say, leave him in the same or better condition as when you first met. Wish him well through words ... and from your heart.

Most men are not good at uncoupling conversations, often preferring to say nothing and disappearing until Thanksgiving, when they suddenly text,

"How are you?" out of the blue.

If your date does take the lead declaring that you're not a fit for him and you agree, then just be grateful that he spared you the talk that you'd prepared, and be happy it set you both free. Don't take it personally. This is not a popularity contest. It's a numbers thing. Get back to your spreadsheet to see who's on the next row.

There were a few times when I thought we could just be friends after dating three times. Although I went out for lunch and stayed in touch for a while with one man, the fact is we didn't make time to prioritize our friendship and rightly so. Frankly, it simply didn't make sense. Save your time for Mr. Right. He will

If your date declares you're not a good fit, and you agree ... don't take it personally. This is not a popularity contest. Get back out there and see who's next!

appreciate the fact that you don't have a stable full of ex-dates that have morphed into pseudo-friends.

SEX

Don't be surprised by the expectation of sex on the third date. This expectation is alive and well. I generally found this to be the case and so did many of my single friends, both men and women.

Sometimes, the decision to embark on sex is very organic and natural, especially if you have lots in common, if there's combustible chemistry and it's obvious that you both want to take it between the sheets to learn whether you're compatible there, too. In those cases, the third date is a crescendo. Be ready for it, freshly shaved legs 'n all.

When you first have sex is completely up to you, of course. Some of you have a loud bell ringing in your head about now, clanging something along the lines of,

Shouldn't we be exclusive first? Shouldn't he have to at least buy me a diamond ring?

No. It's better to figure out sexual compatibility early, before any commitments are made. Chances are you can buy that diamond ring yourself and save yourself the expense and heartache of a divorce. In fact, there's an even bigger urgency to understanding sexual alignment now that you're in the second half of your life. There could be some impediments that you'll want to be aware of and help each other navigate.

Even if you both plan on living to 110, your body may not respond as fluidly as it once did, and his body parts may not rise to full mast like they used to.

If he needs to make love four times a week to make up for the last 10 years of a sexless, failed marriage but you'd rather do the ironing, then it's prudent to figure that out early and save yourselves the trouble of diving into a doomed relationship.

On the other hand, if you are a higher-libido woman, then you'll want to rev up his engines to ensure they rumble the way you like and as often as needed. Fortunately, doctors hand out Viagra and Cialis prescriptions like M&Ms at Halloween. Hold onto your saddles, cowgirls!

But it's not just about virility. It's also about unconventional sexual proclivities, non-traditional preferences and, dare I say, sexual orientation. Sexual orientation can be a fluid thing, especially as midlifers make significant transitions out of marriages, careers and other identities that may not be the "right fit" for them anymore. Don't make assumptions that he's a straight-line heterosexual just because he's a dad or a high school principal. "Mostly straight" is now a distinct sexual identity, too.

Beyond people who are heterosexual for the first part of their lives and then "come out" and switch to a "homosexual" identity, a myriad of other sexual orientations are now being acknowledged to a greater degree. Midnight or morning pillow talk can be a fine time to delicately inquire about non-obvious sexual orientations.

An acquaintance of mine was married with a young child when we first met in a sports club. Then he came out as gay and had various male partners over the course of the next decades. Recently, he fell deeply in love with a woman he met on a vacation, and they married. They now have a blended family with four kids. So, brace yourself to inquire about sexual orientation — what is now called "sexual identity" — the morning after or soon thereafter.

Intimacy was definitely an important variable in my go/no-go decisions. I wanted assurance that we were sexually compatible and that he wasn't going to evangelize anything that I wasn't comfortable with in the bedroom. I didn't want pillow talk about threesomes and I wasn't sure how I'd feel about being in a relationship with a man who was "mostly" heterosexual but occasionally homosexual. I'm not judging, just saying!

If things were going great on the third date for me, clothes got ripped off of each other. If things were going great but I wasn't ready for sex ... let's say that I forgot to shave my legs or I had an early morning commitment that was stressing me ... I'd push my go/no-go decision out by a week or two, but I'd make a point of saying that I was looking forward to spending the night together within the next week or so.

Understandably, he was trying to read me, too. Long periods without intimacy in previous marriages whether by way of "connection breakdown" or protracted illness were an all-too-common narrative that I heard from almost all of the men I dated. Some men figure that they have waited long enough by the third or fourth date. I felt the same way. The clock is ticking, so coy procrastination is not advisable. It can trigger an,

"Oh no, this is not going to happen. I already know how this goes," reaction.

DISCLOSURE DILEMMA

So, do you need to tell him that you're dating other people before you sleep with him? In chapter 6, we started the discussion about contemporaneous dating.

Now, we're talking about disclosure. Funnily enough, no man ever asked me if I was seeing anyone else unless I brought it up.

There are men who dive into intimacy without asking about this because it never dawned on them that you might be dating someone else too. Those men deserve disclosure, otherwise you run the risk of them feeling betrayed, even though it never came up. They should've asked you if it was important to them, but in their defense, I'll say that I met a handful of men who said they never asked me about it because they would never do it. Dating more than one woman at once either violated a personal moral code they had, which I found endearing, or it created too heavy of a mental load.

"I wouldn't even be able to keep the names straight," a civil engineer told me.

These types of men will be surprised when they learn that you've been dating other men. Center yourself if your moral compass starts to feel a bit wobbly at this point. I'll say it again. There is nothing wrong with dating more than one person if you haven't committed to exclusivity. If sexual compatibility is important to you, resist the gravitational "pull" of any "exclusive" dating relationship until after you've been intimate, so you can make a fully informed go/no-go decision.

Timing this type of "dating other men" disclosure requires a certain amount of delicacy and savvy.

When I sensed that the man I was with on our third or fourth date assumed I was dating him exclusively, I proactively disclosed that I was also seeing someone else at some point during the evening, but before intimacy. If I liked him enough, I'd offer that I'd be willing to talk the next day about putting an end to dating the other person, if he felt the same way.

Lastly, the assumption is always that you are practicing safe sex. Maturity does not defend against sexually transmitted diseases. You still need to take precautions, and in my experience, it was always me, the woman, who initiated this conversation. Infection rates for STDs keep climbing among Americans 45

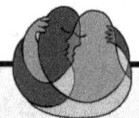

There is nothing wrong with dating more than one person if you haven't committed to exclusivity.

and older, and the increase among older Americans is larger than for the rest of the population.[16] Speak with your physician about the best ways to take precautions, including how to protect yourself against the HPV virus.

CHAPTER 11

REACHING THE ONE YEAR MILESTONE

RELATIONSHIP HOUSEKEEPING

If you transition to an exclusive, loving relationship — you'll be one step further along the road to a long-term commitment. Starting an exclusive relationship typically feels euphoric. It's a milestone to be celebrated and savored.

It should also feel relatively easy to take these next two housekeeping steps:

1. Close your online dating account(s)
2. Stop dating other men

Have an explicit conversation with your sweetheart about how long you each need to do this and then give each other the space to get it done. It shouldn't take

If you don't close your online dating account ... a friend of a friend will surely see it and mention it at some later, extremely inopportune moment.

more than five days, depending on how you want to handle it.

If you don't close your online dating account and ensure that your photos and profile are removed, a friend of a friend will surely see it and mention it at some later, extremely inopportune moment. I promise you that it's sure to get back to your sweetheart and it's bound to happen right after you've had a disagreement. So "sweep your stuff" from the internet and make sure that you haven't inadvertently given permission to the dating site to use your images in any of their advertising. With some sites, there's an "opt out" selection box that you have to choose. Otherwise they still consider you part of their eligible inventory, and continue to use your image in online promotions or in online connections.

Print or save your dating profile on your hard drive before deleting it. The best-case scenario is that your profile can be shared as a humorous relic at your wedding. The other scenario is that you'll update it for a second dating cycle at some future point. I did.

Contact any other men you were dating to let them know you won't be seeing them anymore. For me, this consisted of a phone call to one or two other men. I got a few of those phone calls, too. The men who called me were always gracious, explaining that they had met a lady who was a really good fit and they were now committing to an exclusive relationship. I was truly impressed with the men who made these calls and wished them well.

WHAT TO CALL EACH OTHER

At a certain age, the term "boyfriend" sounds juvenile and odd. "Husband" is an overreach and the word "partner" confuses and understates the romantic aspect, sounding as if you're starting a business or exploring a new sexual orientation.

Frankly, I like these expressions:

- My sweetheart
- My dear-heart

- Mon amour
- My other half

SASHAY AND SAVOR

Take up to one full year to continue to learn each other as "sweethearts" and savor this phase. You need this time to get to know each other in a meaningful way while setting up a framework for a lifetime together. See whether your culture and lifestyles complement each other or combust.

Interact with his family and friends, gently starting to build authentic relationships with those close to him — children, dog, fraternity brothers, golf buddies, church brethren, etc. Notice whether he transforms into someone else when his mother arrives. How is it for you when his guy friends come over for Super Bowl Sunday?

Sashay into the holiday season — Thanksgiving, Valentine's Day, New Year's Eve, and also your respective birthdays. Experience what happens when one or both of you get sick — does he tend to your needs or disappear? Observe whether he's sullen or elated when you leave for a girlfriends' weekend.

What else do you need to know? Does he have a penchant for nature? A need for solitude? How does he think about and manage finances? Experience all the typical ups and downs of a shared life to get to a place of knowing each other so that you can make a decision about a lifetime relationship with confidence. According to relationship experts like the Gottmans,

> *"Successful long-term relationships are created through small words, small gestures, and small acts."*[17]

DATE NIGHTS

A regular rhythm of "date nights" is invaluable to any relationship, regardless of whether you are in your first year as sweethearts or have been married for five years. Over time, the pragmatic and transactional aspects of relationships creep in and dampen that initial intractable burning love.

A fair and fun way to approach date nights is to alternate hosting them like this:

1. The host plans, executes and pays for the entire date.

2. The host unilaterally picks the activity — one that he or she enjoys without buy-in from the invitee.

3. The invitee is obliged to show up joyfully with an open mind and participate without reservation.

I am a huge fan of date nights because you get to continue learning about each other by sharing your favorite activities without overcomplicating anything. Plus, the host is generally very enthusiastic about engineering activities that they love instead of stressing and guessing about the invitee's potential reaction or preferences. Take limitations into account, of course. Don't take your sweetheart horseback riding if he's allergic to horses or has a back problem.

There's no need to be extravagant if it's not in the budget. Creativity is what matters. I once dated a man who was between jobs with limited income but he had a pro fly-fishing instructor certification. Although we didn't live near any fly-fishing rivers when we were involved with each other, he planned a lovely "date" evening. He took a bottle of red wine and two of his fishing rods down to a grassy public park at sunset, and he taught me how to tie flies and cast the line. I appreciated the poetic time in nature.

Lastly, don't get ahead of yourself in this first year of exclusive dating. Enjoy the romance, but keep your independence and identity separate. Don't take on wifely duties and don't move in together. If you decide that the relationship isn't working and you plan to break up, it'll be harder and more complicated if you're living together. The centrifugal force is simply stronger once the two of you create a home.

By all means, don't wait the full year to uncouple if "fatal flaws" surface sooner. Although both of you are capable of evolving, let's face it. It's unlikely that either of you is going to change in substantial ways unless you do some deep personal development work. Ideally that kind of work is done solo, *before* you start dating seriously. However, if after one year you strongly feel that he's the right-fit guy, then take it to the next level and move in with each other, get married and all of that wonderful stuff.

CHAPTER 12

BREAKING UP AND TAKING A BREAK

FATAL FLAWS

Fatal flaws are big things, not little ones. These are your non-negotiables. You predefined what "fatal flaw" means to you as part of figuring out what your online search criteria was when you started online dating. Often, you'll add or even subtract a few non-obvious ones along the way, too. Sometimes, you'll think he doesn't have any but then, surprise! A fatal flaw emerges from the shadows.

For me, fatal flaws included: active alcoholism, a pattern of angry outbursts or rage, not paying income tax, a porn addiction, brazen flirting (but not with me), an inability to support himself (unless he was sick), and a scarcity mentality — people whose mindset stems from a place of lack; e.g., they continually feel that there will never be "enough" money, food, love or attention paid to them. These flaws aren't all of equal significance, but they are my deal breakers nonetheless. I'd rather be alone than put up with any them.

I recall a particularly charismatic boyfriend who, to my knowledge, never cheated on me but was a relentless flirt. He'd flick subtle yet piercing glances at women across the theater while holding my hand. Then suddenly during intermission, women would appear at our side, sprinkling chatty details about where they lived like breadcrumbs on the path to Grandma's house. This pattern was so nuanced that it took me a while to catch on, but over the course of more than a few buzzkill evenings, I figured it out. The ensuing brain rush and drama that he experienced, were part of an adrenalin addiction that would require more than a few couples counseling sessions. I broke up with him. It was hard.

HOW TO UNCOUPLE AND MEAN IT

The one-year mark is a milestone at which you should still be clear about your relationship goals and feel confident that you are tracking in that direction.

Check in with yourself. If "fatal flaws" surfaced, pull the plug to begin the dating cycle anew.

If you're breaking up, be clear with yourself about the reasons why. Write them all out. Then clarify and distill them into no more than three reasons, although one reason is good enough. Pretend that you are headed to a therapist whose hourly rate is hundreds of dollars. It behooves you to be honest and concise so that you can spend most of the therapy hour pressure testing the reasons. And if you do in fact head to a therapist, then good for you! A little validation can help, too.

If you've done this reasonably well, you'll fully understand why you're breaking up. If you know the exact reasons why you're breaking up, then uncoupling will not only be easier for you but it'll be digestible for him. This is an important process because after investing so much emotion and time into the budding relationship that you're about to break off, there will come a time when you will churn and second guess yourself, spiraling into a vortex of doubt or regret. Having the exact reasons as to why you broke up at hand, can help you stand by your decision later.

Next, plan a time to talk to him. In my view, it is never acceptable to break up with someone by text or email. Talk to him in person unless you're not in the same city. I confess that I've broken up over the phone while traveling. I simply didn't have a reasonable face-to-face opportunity on the horizon, but couldn't "pretend" anymore.

And in case he tries to talk you out of it, tell him that you've already activated your online dating account again. An accepting silence will likely ensue.

HE BREAKS UP

It's a blow to the ego if he breaks up with you, but it's not the end of the world. If it's not a surprise, ask yourself what your take-aways are. Just because he broke up does not mean there's something wrong with you or that online dating doesn't work. You didn't have the right-fit man, but ask yourself:

"Were we trending in the right direction?"

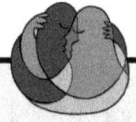

It's a blow to the ego if he breaks up with you, but it's not the end of the world.

Give yourself some credit. Celebrate the little "wins." The big win will come soon enough. Go back to your drawing board and set an intention for a guy who is a better fit than you even imagined when you first started dating. Take your profile out of the drawer. Remember, I suggested earlier that you print it. Dating is a numbers game.

TAKE A BREAK

Take time off as needed. You might not require it, especially if you were experiencing a lot of conflict with each other early on, or if you never connected as deeply as you'd hoped you would.

On the other hand, if you feel like your heart was broken, don't deny that you may not be ready to date right away. Take a trip or two, sign up for a rejuvenating retreat, but get moving in a gentle, restorative way to recalibrate your energy so that you re-center. Avoid rebound relationships. Your goal should be to bring your best, most optimistic self into the dating arena … again.

CHAPTER 13

NOW YOU HAVE GAME

Once you've dated a full cycle, you have "game"! You'll be in an incredibly good position, able to harness everything you learned during your first dating cycle and you'll be more confident, discerning and optimistic. You'll no longer shadow box with urban legends and unfounded fears about online dating and you'll be able to spot a scammer a mile away. In all probability, you'll have had some wonderful times, met some interesting, fun men and learned about some local venues you never knew existed.

The next time around, set your sights even higher. Why? Because your view of the world has expanded. You'll be wiser and because you…can. You'll know what dating looks like at this life stage and you'll understand how to build a great profile that attracts the kind of man you are looking for. You'll be pragmatic about

This next time around, set your sights even higher.
Why?
Because you're wiser and because ... you can.

how to move forward with this process. Embrace the fact that you live in an age and culture where you can date easily, openly and freely without any cultural or social repercussions.

I dated two full cycles. They spanned three years — 38 months. The first time, I did online dating for four months, until a traffic jam built up, but by then I'd dated eight guys. That eighth man was someone I really enjoyed for many reasons. One big reason was because I felt so adored. He made me laugh a lot, and he told wonderful stories.

I spent 18 months with that charming Southern gentleman, but the last six months were rocky. He broke up with me twice. We went to couples counseling but there were value differences we couldn't seem to bridge, plus a fatal flaw had surfaced. Finally, I broke up with him.

When I embarked on the second cycle, I was confident about the process and more clear about the amount of time and energy it was going to take. Again, it took approximately four months and it was that eighth man who captured my heart, a smoldering, bearded Argentinian-American who skis!

Although I was using Match, I'd been experimenting with Bumble, since I was intrigued by the fact that the woman has 24 hours to make the first move when there's a connection. We met on Bumble and moved in together after one year. To my surprise, serendipity struck yet again when I found out that his physics thesis had been: "1+1> 2."

Eight might not be a magic number, but it's a decent goal post. It might be more or less for you, but don't even think about giving up before you've dated eight men. Dating is not rocket science but it's best done methodically, understanding that it involves work just as if you were looking for your dream job.

Among all the dating women I've spoken with, the ones who felt joyful about the dating process and seemed to have success with it said that they treated it like a business AND they set out to have fun. They did!

Don't be dogmatic about which sites you use. Using at least one paid site made the most sense to me and

Women who felt joyful about the dating process and seemed to have success with it treated it like a business and set out to have fun.

I heard from other women that Match, a paid site, seemed to have the most inventory and was a go-to site for the men, too. Almost everyone experimented with sites though.

One last thing. Your attitude matters tremendously. When I first started dating, I did an informal interview with a lady who told me that she dated for 11 years and had so much fun that she thought she'd never get married. Although she is happily married now as a result of her dating journey, I cherished her mindset and the joyful lens that she imparted on me for my dating journey.

When I conducted research interviews for this book, the women I spoke with who seemed to have the most success online dating, had an expectation of having fun. Some said that they even went out with men who they knew were not great fits, but because they were comedic or interesting, they went for fun anyway. A vibrant woman with an open mind and a fun spirit, is alluring.

Your thoughts transmit energy — curious, fair-minded, confident, sensual...or the opposite — narrow minded, high-handed, not worthy, disappointed. Practice loving kindness on the dating front — towards "him" and towards yourself.

So sharpen up your profile and refine your list of critical requirements if you're embarking on round two. I bet they've changed! And remember these seven guidelines:

1. Use a **paid** dating site.
2. Push to the **phone**, limit texting.
3. **Meet eight** men in person.
4. Commit to **3 dates.**
5. Be your **best self,** every time.
6. **Let** him take the **lead**.
7. Pressure test a **right-fit** relationship for up to **one year.**

I wish for you an invigorating, joyful dating journey. May each in-person encounter add something interesting, soulful or juicy to your life until you find your "stop" in the arms of a right-fit man.

ENDNOTES

1 Rosenfeld, Michael J., Reuben, Thomas J., and Hausen, Sonia (2019). "Disintermediating Your Friends." Accepted for publication. https://web.stanford.edu/~mrosenfe/Rosenfeld_et_al_Disintermediating_Friends.pdf

2 "Online dating has jumped among adults under age 25 as well as those in their late 50s and early 60s." "15% of American Adults Have Used Online Dating Sites or Mobile Dating Apps," Aaron Smith. Pew Research Center, Feb 29, 2016. http://www.pewresearch.org/fact-tank/2016/02/29/5-facts-about-online-dating/

3 Most popular online dating apps in the United States as of March 2019, by audience size (in millions)." Statista. https://www.statista.com/statistics/826778/most-popular-dating-apps-by-audience-size-usa/

4 Zoosk home page, June 19, 2019, https://www.zoosk.com/

5 "More Men Use Dating Apps Than Women," Laura Stampler. Time, February 17, 2015. http://time.com/3711902/men-use-dating-apps-more-tinder/

6 "… they often lack the amount of matches necessary to provide the dates women over 40 need, despite what they promise prior too signing up." "Do Matchmakers for Women over 40 Actually Work? The Unfortunate Truth Behind 'Matchmaking,'" Joshua Pompey. Huffington Post, February 9 2017. https://www.huffpost.com/entry/do-matchmakers-for-women-over-40-actually-work-the_b_589cdf6de4b0e172783a9a22

7 "Best Matchmaking Services," Mark Brooks. Consumer Affairs, January 28, 2019. https://www.consumeraffairs.com/dating_services/matchmaker/#matchmaking-services-cost

8 As of April 2017, the leading dating website in the United States was Match.com with a U.S. online user awareness reach of 67 percent. Closest competitors were eHarmony.com, ChristianMingle and dating app Tinder. "On-line Dating in the United States — Statistics & Facts," J. Clem-

ent. Statista, March 20, 2019. https://www.statista.com/topics/2158/online-dating/

9 "Senior sex: Tips for older men," Mayo Clinic Staff. Mayo Clinic, July 14, 2017. https://www.mayoclinic.org/healthy-lifestyle/sexual-health/in-depth/senior-sex/art-20046465

10 "The Gray Gender Gap: Older Women are Likely to Go it Alone," Paula Span. *New York Times,* Oct 11, 2016 https://www.nytimes.com/2016/10/11/health/marital-status-elderly-health.html

11 "Women can still expect to live longer than men: 81.1 vs. 76.1 years." "US Life Expectancy Drops Second Year in a Row." Ben Tinker. CNN, Dec 21, 2018. https://www.cnn.com/2017/12/21/health/us-life-expectancy-study/index.html

12 Bumble (https://bumble.com/) is a female-founded dating site where the woman has 24 hours to make the first move. Although the profiles are short and depend more on pictures, it's an exciting model that favors action-oriented women who want to control the initial outreach. Note that some men who use Bumble, simply "choose" by right swiping all women in their inventory.

13 "Chemistry & Dating," Mary Johnston-Gerard. Datingtips.Match.com. https://datingtips.match.com/chemistry-dating-6724139.html

14 A scientist who's worked at Tinder and Bumble says too many people make the same mistake in their dating profile photo," Shana Lebowitz. Business Insider, May 12, 2018. https://www.businessinsider.com/tinder-bumble-scientist-smile-online-dating-photo-2018-5

15 Why Married Women and Men Are Visiting Online Chat Rooms for Dates: Extramarital affairs are rising on the Internet," Leonard Holmes. VeryWellMind, updated April 09, 2019. https://www.verywellmind.com/online-dating-is-popular-with-married-men-and-women-2330727?print

16 "STD Rates Keep Rising for Older Adults," Randy Lilleston. AARP, September 28, 2017. https://www.aarp.org/health/conditions-treatments/info-2017/std-exposure-rises-older-adults-fd.html

17 "We've Been Studying Couples for 40 Years — Here's What We Learned About Improving Your Odds of Lasting Love," John Gottman, Julie Schwartz Gottman, Doug Abrams and Rachel Carlton Abrams. Thrive Global, February 12, 2019. https://thriveglobal.com/stories/couples-relationship-therapists-lasting-love-advice/amp/ Excerpted from *Eight Dates: Essential Conversations for a Lifetime of Love,* John Gottman, Julie Schwartz Gottman, Doug Abrams, Rachel Carlton Abrams (Workman Publishing, 2019).

ACKNOWLEDGEMENTS

Deeply grateful to Carlos Gonzalez as we celebrate our third anniversary with love in the Canadian wilderness. You commit exquisitely well.

Sincere thanks to Robin Surface, amazing publisher, Frances Archer O'Cherony, uplifting editor, Chris Molineaux, digital quarterback, Nicola Oldham, decades-long writing cheerleader, Susan Burak, law school alum and lifelong literary exploring partner, Yardena Vener, law school alum and transition touchstone, Trisha Emish, truth teller and early reviewer, Lynn Bodfish, Cathy Boyer & Sandi Bacon, my CA life-stage mountaineers, Dr. Tessa Warshaw, fire-igniter on the road ahead, Dr. Lisa Large & William Pickard III, providers of valuable input, Roni Erikson, health nurturer, and the Lunch Dames of Houston.

Gratitude and shout-outs to my loving family: Gabriele Hile, Nicola, Jeremy, Daniel and Julian Oldham, Cathy Donald, Mark, Alysha and Jenny Hile.

One + One >2

Sincere appreciation to the couples who were (and still are) my role models for lasting, romantic commitment: L. Lanius, the Horsts, the Weiners, the Cannizzaro's, the Rotwein/Pappas', the Halbert/Elder's, and the Tetzlaff's.

ABOUT THE AUTHOR

Christiane Hile is a Canadian-American. She was a litigation attorney for eight years after graduating with a law degree from the University of British Columbia, and a BA from the University of Victoria. Ever-curious and optimistic, she purposefully transitioned to product marketing and market research in the technology sector, spending 13 years in California and five in Texas. This is her first book. She lives in Houston, Texas with her sweetheart and standard poodle.

TO STAY ABREAST
OR TO GET MORE INFORMATION
ABOUT ONLINE DATING FOR WOMEN
OVER 50, VISIT:

https://ChristianeHile.com

www.ingramcontent.com/pod-product-compliance
Lightning Source LLC
Chambersburg PA
CBHW052147110526
44591CB00012B/1890